APR 2 1 2006

D1451812

DISCARD

A GUIDE TO BEGINNER

TUMBLING

A GUIDE TO BEGINNER

TUMBLING

MIKE FERRALLI

American Literary Press, Inc.
Five Star Special Edition
Baltimore, Maryland

A GUIDE TO BEGINNER TUMBLING

Copyright (C) 2003 US Tumblers Inc.

<u>DISCLAIMER</u>

The information set forth within this book is intended for persons who have some prior experience in cheerleading and/or gymnastics. The information provided is believed to be reliable, but US Tumblers, Inc. makes no guarantees as to its reliability and effectiveness. Some of the material provided herein may not be suitable for all persons. Its appropriateness may vary depending on the participant's age, weight, height, fitness level, health, athletic ability, experience and other factors. No person should attempt any of the movements or implement any of the material/programs provided herein without first consulting a physician, nutritionist and personal trainer. Any implementation of the material contained within should be under direct supervision by a trained professional/experienced coach who is personally present at all times. US Tumblers, Inc. specifically and expressly disclaims any and all responsibility and/or liability for use of the information contained within this book. By following any of the material contained within, the participant assumes any and all risk and liability of his /her performance of the material contained within.

Library of Congress
Cataloging - in-Publication Data
ISBN 1-56167-798-1

Library of Congress Card Catalog Number:
2003091523

Second Printing, 2005

Published by

American Literary Press
Five Star Special Edition
8019 Belair Road, Suite 10
Baltimore, Maryland 21236

Manufactured in the United States of America

COACHING TIPS

This book covers the drills and techniques that teach body control, body awareness, and tumbling. Safety information as well as some nutritional and conditioning information is also included.

This first thing to understand as a coach is that you are in charge and are ultimately responsible for a team's success or failure. Discipline provides the key to your success as a coach. A disciplined team has learning potential. If discipline is lacking, and the athletes lack definitive guidance, their performance and learning potential will be severely compromised. It is very important that a coach sets both goals and boundaries for the athletes to ensure they are learning and performing at his/her maximum potential.

Another important aspect to a team's success is motivation. Athletes need to be excited about what they are doing. You need to provide them with both motivation and discipline. Unfortunately there is no set way to accomplish this. Every team is different as well as each individual athlete on the team. You must determine what motivates both your individual athletes and the team as a whole.

Below is a list of several steps to follow to make a solid foundation to build your team on.

1) Practices are mandatory and should not be missed without a valid excuse and prior notification.
2) Tardiness to practices and games should not be tolerated without prior notification and a valid excuse.
3) Do not tolerate disruptive behavior, talking, goofing-off, disrespect towards you or other athletes.
4) Set goals and standards for the athletes and the team that they must meet throughout the year. These goals should be high but attainable in a reasonable amount of time.(examples: athletes must have standing backhand springs by [November] and standing back tucks by [January]; must have team double base extensions by [September] and team libs by [October] and extension 360s by [October].
5) Set up a strength and conditioning program that the athletes must follow on their own outside of practice. Test the athletes every so often on certain conditioning exercises to ensure there is improvement and they are following the workout program.
6) Have the athletes stretch and condition both before and after practice under your supervision.
7) You must instill in your athletes the expectation of being good. If they believe that they can accomplish something, then they can. Don't allow them to not believe they are capable of anything. Your athletes need to believe in themselves and each other and expect to hit both the basic and higher level skills. They need to have the attitude of a champion, no matter what level they are.
8) Do not be afraid to push your athletes hard. You want to have athletes that want to be there and want to be good. Being good is a matter of hard work. At the same time you must make sure practices are fun as well as productive. It is okay to have extremely hard practices as well as just fun practices. The majority of practices should be a combination of the two, hard but fun.

9) Have the team do drills and play games that encourage teamwork and team cohesiveness. The better a team works together and gets along, the more they will accomplish and the harder they will work to meet both your and his/her goals.

10) Remember that coaching is not a total dictatorship. You need to take into account what your athletes want to accomplish with the team. They need to know that you respect them, their thoughts and ideas. This will promote their respect for you and allow you to instill the discipline that they need. With both respect and discipline, the goals that you and the team set can be accomplished. Respect is very important for both sides, without it, discipline is worthless.

STRENGTH & CONDITIONING, HEALTH & NUTRITION

Most cheerleaders want to be considered athletes. They want the same respect other sports get. Unfortunately, they have a misconception of what being an athlete actually is. They believe that performing athletic skills and/or tricks is all that is involved in being an athlete. This is far from the truth. The most important aspect of being an athlete is getting in and staying in shape, and increasing physical strength. The majority of an athlete's time is spent training their bodies to be stronger, have more endurance, and be more proficient at their sport. The actual playing of a game and/or performance of a routine is a very small part of being an athlete. Most cheerleaders who want to be athletes do not truly understand the hard work and dedication it takes to be a good athlete. Lifting weights and running are very important parts of being an athlete. This will develop both strength and endurance which are essential for any athlete.

Apart from the training in the gym, and at practice, there is something that is even more important to be a good athlete. It is also one of the most basic of human needs - eating. Proper nutrition and eating habits are vital for anyone who wishes to train and be an athlete. If one does not eat properly, their bodies will break down and they will not have the energy to train and grow. Improper eating habits are detrimental to an athlete's health and safety. It's a coach's responsibility to ensure that athletes understand how important it is to eat properly and train their bodies. All coaches should bring in certified nutritionists and strength coaches to work with their team regularly.

SAFETY CONSIDERATIONS

Before your athlete start to learn how to tumble, it is important he/she understand that any activity involving height and/or motion can involve severe injury, including permanent paralysis or death. Therefore, it is very important that both the coach and athlete take steps to ensure his/her safety. The first step is quite simple. It involves the athlete's paying attention to what is going on around them and to what they are doing. Also, being aware of what others are doing so that he/she does not get in anyone else's way. This will prevent both he/she and the other person from becoming injured. Athletes also need to fully concentrate on what they are doing and give it 150% effort. If they do drills/skills lackadaisically, they will greatly increase the chance of injury to themselves. Since most tumbling skills involve the athlete being upside down, landing on one's head is very possible. This will most likely happen if an athlete bails on a skill and/or does not give it a total effort. Bailing out of a skill is usually the result of an athlete letting fear and emotion get the best of him/her. The body/mind resorts to its natural instincts when fear takes control. Unfortunately, the natural instinct is to open up and come out of a skill. This is very dangerous since landing on one's head is the most likely outcome. This is why doing drills repetitiously is so important. Drills train the body/mind how to react. They teach you new instincts. A good example of this is tripping while you walk. You do not think about how to keep your balance, you simply react. This is because you have learned the instinct of how to keep your balance. It is not a natural instinct, it is learned through experience. Your body/mind uses this learned instinct to balance you. The same will happen with one's gymnastics skills/drills. By doing the drills and skills correctly and repetitiously, your body will learn instinct on how to stay safe and not bail on the skill/drill. These new instincts will help an athlete stay safe. A rule that should be instilled in your athletes is that he/she never comes out of any skill/drill. This is not to say that if he/she is doing a round-off back handspring back tuck, that they cannot stop after the round-off or the handspring. It does mean that he/she cannot stop midway through the round-off, or the back handspring or the back tuck. This is true for any skill/drill. Staying in control of one's body and not bailing out of a skill/drill is a very important safety aspect. When an athlete loses control and lets fear take control, an injury will most likely to occur.

Some simple skills an athlete can do will also help prevent injuries. A forward or backward roll are two perfect examples. A roll is extremely basic and most everybody has done it while they were growing up. One tucks the chin to the chest, and then pulls the legs to the body and rolls either forward or backward. These two simple skills can save an athlete a lot of pain and injury. For example, in a handstand, if an athlete starts to fall over, instead of getting loose and panicking, an athlete should stay tight and forward roll out of it. As he/she falls over, he/she tucks the chin to the chest and slowly bends the arms lowering the body to the ground. The goal is to place the upper back/shoulders gently onto the ground and then roll out of it by tucking the legs. If the athlete panics and gets loose, he/she will either slam his/her back and/or head on the ground. Again, staying tight and in control of the body is the key.

Another example is when an athlete is falling backwards. The natural instinct is to reach the arms behind him/her to catch oneself. **This is extremely dangerous because a broken elbow can very easily occur.** When an athlete puts his/her arms behind them to catch him/herself, the arms are in a position where any force on the hands causes the arms to lock and hyper-extend. If an athlete falls and places enough force on the arm(s), which is actually not that much, the elbow will lock, hyper-extend, dislocate and/or break. This is an extremely painful and gruesome injury. In a lot of cases, depending on the severity of the injury, the elbow will never fully heal. Preventing this injury is extremely easy. NEVER PLACE YOUR ARMS BEHIND YOU TO CATCH YOURSELF WIIEN FALLINC!! Instcad, roll backwards out of it. Any time you are falling backwards, for whatever reason, simply place your arms across your chest, sit to the ground and roll. This will prevent any type of arm injury which is very common when trying to catch yourself. By simply rolling either forward or backward out of certain drills/skills instead of getting loose and coming out of the skill/drill, one can prevent a lot of injuries. **Most injuries can be prevented by the athlete simply staying tight and not bailing out of a skill/drill.** By teaching your athletes the following, you will greatly reduce the likelihood of an athlete becoming injured.

1) Pay attention to their environment and what is going on around them.
2) Have total concentration on what they are doing and give it their total effort.
3) Spend the time learning drills and skills correctly and do not rush into doing something they're not ready for.
4) Never bailout midway through a skill.
5) Stay tight and in control; never let fear take control.
6) Learn how to fall safely (roll out of a fall or over rotation).
7) Never use the arms to catch themselves when falling backward.

Safety should always be foremost and utmost on the coach's and athlete's minds. As soon as someone becomes complacent about what they're doing, the probability of an injury will greatly increase.

Other aspects of safety include ensuring that athletes are training in a safe environment with proper equipment and matting. Inspecting the equipment they are using for damage, excess wear, tears, breaks etc. Ensure equipment is well maintained and in good shape. Make sure your athletes receive proper training from trained professionals. Never try to teach something you are not qualified or able to teach. These are by no means the only safety considerations that both you and your athletes need to consider. However, they do cover the most common areas. By following these steps and suggestions, you can reduce the chances that one of your athletes will become injured.

TUMBLING

NOTE: All training should be performed with proper gymnastics/cheerleading equipment/matting. Each drill requires different safety equipment/matting that should be used as required. **This manual was written, keeping in mind, that most schools have very limited gymnastics/cheerleading matting. The drills covered reflect that.** *It's very important that you constantly remind athletes that learning tumbling is a long and involved process and requires lots of time and effort. Athletes shouldn't get frustrated when learning a skill doesn't happen over night. It may take many months to learn and years to perfect some skills.*

As cheerleading develops as a sport, tumbling is more and more becoming both an integral and important part of it. Unfortunately, it is one of the most difficult aspects to learn. There are two basic forms of tumbling in the cheerleading world. The first is "chunk and throw" tumbling, and the second is gymnastics tumbling.

As its name suggests, "chunk and throw" tumbling means chunking the tumbling skill just so the athlete gets over. It utilizes very little technique, isn't clean looking, and can be very detrimental to the athlete's physical health. A lot of cheerleaders want to learn a handspring or standing tuck as fast as possible and not worry about proper technique. This is how the "chunk and throw" method was started. People wanting to learn tumbling as quickly as possible without concern for cleanliness or technique. There are several downsides to learning tumbling skills via the "chunk and throw" method.

1) Skills aren't very clean, are sloppy looking, and lack fluidness.
2) The skill has very little power and requires a lot more effort to perform than it would with good technique.
3) Putting multiple skills together such as a back-handspring back tuck becomes very difficult due to the lack of power and bad technique.
4) The athlete's body takes excessive pounding due to the lack of technique. This can cause the athlete physical injury in the future such as tendinitis, stress fractures, joint deterioration, muscle strains, etc.
5) The difficulty of skills an athlete can learn as well as the time it takes to learn them will be adversely affected.

Ultimately, "chunk and throw" tumbling is not a valid form of tumbling. It's the result of coaches teaching skills they are not qualified to teach and athletes rushing to learn a skill without proper technique.

Gymnastics tumbling is the only correct form of tumbling that should be taught. Unfortunately, there are not many cheerleading coaches that are qualified to coach gymnastics tumbling. Also, most cheerleaders are unwilling to put the time and effort into learning tumbling the correct way. It's your responsibility as a coach to ensure your athletes learn tumbling the correct way. Contained within are the basic drills and techniques for beginner tumbling.

There are three very important aspects to tumbling no matter what level gymnast/tumbler you are.

1) Strength and conditioning
2) Body control and body awareness
3) Drills, drills, and more drills to lcarn proper technique

These three guidelines are the key to both basic and advanced tumbling skills. The first one refers to an athlete's physical strength and endurance. If the athlete has the strength to manipulate his/her body, then he/she can learn how to tumble. They also need to have enough endurance to perform the skills without becoming exhausted while performing them. The second refers to making the body do what it needs to do. Performing tumbling skills is only possible when an athlete can manipulate his/her body into the correct positions that the skills require. In other words, if you cannot control your body and make it do what is required to perform a skill, then performance of that skill is much harder, if not impossible. The third aspect is simple. Learn tumbling skills in the correct manner. When proper technique is learned and used, then performance of the skill requires less effort and energy. Proper technique also generates speed and power which is used to do multiple skill passes. Power and speed also leads to the ability of advanced skill performance which require both speed and power.

The most important thing to remember and stress to the athletes while they are learning how to tumble is strict form. While they are doing their drills it is important that they do not cheat, but do the drills correctly. Cheating and not doing the drills correctly lead to bad habits, and in the long-run, make learning harder. Tumbling is a matter of putting many drills together to form larger and larger drills/skills. The easiest way to perform these drills/skills is through muscle memory. Muscle memory is formed when the muscles in one's body do the same thing over and over again. Walking, talking, and breathing are great examples of muscle memory. All of these activities occur without much thought or concentration at all. Our bodies have done these activities for so long that the muscles know how to do them without concentration. The only thing our brain has to do is decide to do it.

When learning how to tumble, one wants to make skill performance second nature to them, just like walking and talking. This is achieved through correct, repetitive drill performance. Strict adherence to form is very, very important. *NOTE: The strict form covered/used in the beginner drills/skills is maintained in every subsequent drill/skill whether mentioned or not. The beginner drills that teach body control and awareness should never be abandoned. The stronger an athlete's basics are, the stronger his/her more advanced skills will be. One can always improve his/her basics.*

A couple of basic concepts that your athletes need to understand is, what is an arch and a pike. An arch occurs due to the lack of body control, tightness and good technique. Though a pike is a legitimate gymnastics position, it is not used in the skills that are covered in this book, therefore it is an incorrect position. To understand what an arch is, have an athlete lie on his/her back with legs together and arms stretched over his/her head and stay loose and relaxed. Then stand over the athlete, grab his/her waist and lift it about a foot off the floor. The Athlete's hands and feet should still be on the floor. This is an arch (See Fig 1), which is different from a tight-arch which will be covered later in the book.

Fig 1: Arch position

An arch cannot occur in an athlete if their stomach muscles are tight. A pike is just the opposite. Have an athlete standup straight, then bend over and touch their toes keeping their legs straight. Their buttocks should be in the air; ask them to try and squeeze their buttocks. They will NOT be able to. Next have them stand up and try to squeeze their buttocks again. They will be able to. If an athlete's buttocks is tight, bending over is impossible. So is landing bent over as a lot of cheerleaders do when they perform a handspring.

The most important and fundamental position in gymnastics is the handstand. To do a handstand correctly, it is very important that the athletes keep both their stomachs and buttocks tight, with their head between their arms. There are several drills that lead up to this position. The first is the push-up drill.

A gymnastics push-up is done differently than most people would think. To start, place the hands on the floor directly under your shoulders. Raise the upper back/shoulders towards the ceiling. Keep the lower back and buttocks straight and flat with legs tight together. The buttocks should be squeezed and tight at all times. This curved position of the chest and stomach with the flat lower back and buttocks is referred to as the *hollow-position*. To perform the pushup one should hold this body position. Only the elbows should bend. Make sure there is no flecture(bending) in the lower back nor should the buttocks be in the air while the push-up is performed (See Fig. 2-5). This form places a great amount of pressure on the abdominal muscles. This will force the body to learn how to control and squeeze the abdominal muscles as well as strengthening them. The athlete should go as close to the ground as possible without sacrificing correct form.

Fig 2: Correct start position (hollow push-up position)

Fig 3: Correct finish position

Fig 4: Incorrect; buttocks is in the air

Fig 5: Incorrect; arching of the back

The next drill that strengthens and teaches abdominal control is the crunch drill. First, the athlete should lie on his/her back with the arms completely stretched back over the head. The shoulders/biceps should be against the ears; this position for the head is called the *neutral-position*. The legs should be tight together, toes pointed, ankles together, buttocks tight and shoulders shrugged (See Fig 6-8).

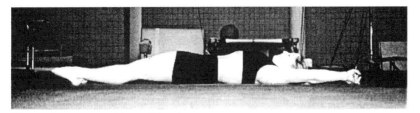

Fig 6: Correct position; side view

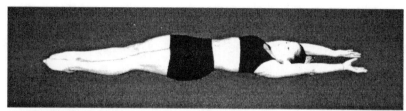
Fig 7: Correct position; top angle view

Fig 8: Incorrect position; lower back arched up off floor

To perform the crunch, use the abdominal muscles to lift the shoulder blades up off the ground. Make sure the arms and head are not lifted independently of the chest, and the chin is not tucked to the chest. The athlete should constantly face the ceiling. This drill should be performed slowly and meticulously (See Fig 9-11). It is training the body as a whole to stay tight. It works the arms, shoulders, legs, toes, buttocks, abs, etc. Shoulders need not come up off the ground more than 2-3 inches. The athlete should come up and hold in the up position for 2-3 seconds, then come back down. The entire time they are doing this drill, they need to keep their entire body tight.

Fig 9: Correct start position

Fig 10: Correct end position

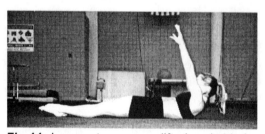
Fig 11: Incorrect; arms are lifted and chin is tucked

Another drill for a handstand that concentrates on the buttocks are <u>leg-raises</u>. This can be done either on the ground or a raised surface like a bench or panel-mat. First, the athlete needs to lie on hi/her stomach using the arms to either hold the sides of the bench/mat or have them stretched out over the head if lying on the floor. Keeping the legs straight and locked together with toes pointed, an athlete uses hi/her buttocks muscles to lift the legs up of the floor/mat hold for 2-3 seconds then relax (See Fig. 12-13). To make this exercise harder the athlete can wear ankle weights, hold a weight between his/her feet, or have a buddy push down on his/her legs while he/she perform the exercise.

Fig 12: Correct start position

Fig 13: Correct end position

The last basic exercise that should be performed before the handstand is the kick drill. To perform this drill the athlete gets a chair, bench or mat and bends over and places his/her hands on it. Their upper back is rounded just like in the push-up drill. His/her arms should be straight and legs should be in a small lunge (See Fig. 14). Using the back leg, which is straight, he/she kicks it up into the air and pushes through the toes of the front leg to raise the hips up off the ground (See Fig. 15-17). It is important that there is no flecture in the lower back while the athlete kicks. The rotation point of the body should be the shoulders. The hips should rise up off the floor over the shoulders. As the athlete becomes more and more comfortable and adept at this drill he/she can increase how hard they kick and how high they go.

Fig 14: Correct start position

Fig 15: Kicking back leg and pushing through front leg

Fig 16: Correct end position

Fig 17: Incorrect; head out and back arched

Finally, it is time to put all the drills together into a handstand. The athlete wants to start in a lunge with his/her arms up over his/her head; *head is in the neutral-position* (See Fig. 18). Reaching down to the floor, placing the hands close to the wall, they kick the back leg to raise the hips over the shoulders just like in the kick drill. As the body rises, he/she wants to be sure to keep the buttocks tight and shoulders shrugged, chest, back and stomach in the *hollow-position* (See Fig. 19-22). When first performing a handstand it is suggested performing it against a wall. Once they feel comfortable with it and can stabilize and balance themselves, the can do it in the middle of the floor.

Fig 18: Start position

Fig 19: Reaching to floor while kicking up

Fig 20: Kicking up to wall

Fig 21: Correct end position (handstand)

Fig 22: Incorrect end position; head is out and back is arched

If the athlete has a hard time feeling what the handstand is supposed to feel like, have them get into the *hollow push-up position*. A buddy needs to grab the athlete's ankles and lift them up over his/her shoulders to a handstand position. While the athlete's feet are being raised, it is extremely important that there is no flecture in the lower back, the head rotates to the *neutral-position,* the shoulders stay shrugged and the legs stay tight together and toes are pointed.

For an athlete to be able to balance in a handstand his/her body must stay perfectly tight. The point of rotation in a hand stand is the wrist. Just as someone uses his/her heels and toes to balance while standing upright, one uses his/her palms and fingers to balance in a handstand. The balance point in a handstand is just past vertical. The athlete wants to have his/her body leaning more over the fingers than the palm of the hand (See Fig. 23-27). This allows one to use the fingers to push through the floor and stop from falling over just as he/she uses his/her toes to stop from falling over while standing upright. With enough practice the point of balance can be achieved with little compensation from the fingers.

Fig 23: Not far enough over hands

Fig 24: Correct handstand position with head inline

Fig 25: Correct handstand with head out

Fig 26: To far past vertical

Fig 27: Head too far out, creates an arch in lower back

Once a handstand has been successfully achieved with consistency, the athlete can begin to learn a handspring, a back tuck, a round-off, etc. The drills used to learn other tumbling skills are a modified version of the handstand drills.

NOTE: There are literally thousands of drills that can be used in conjunction with or in lieu of the drills contained within this manual, far to many too cover all of them. This manual only covers the most common and basic drills used to teach tumbling skills. Some athletes may need additional drills and instruction to learn how to tumble. If you have an athlete that is having difficulty learning , consult a trained gymnastics coach for additional assistance.

BACK HANDSPRING

The first thing after the handstand that one needs to learn is how to snap down properly out of the handstand; this is called the snap drill. Lying on the ground in the same position as the crunch drill, the athlete pushes hi/her buttocks 1-2 inches up off the floor. This is known as the *tight-arch position* (See Fig. 28) which is much different from the arched position discussed earlier. Its very important that the strict form used for the crunch drill be adhered to, which included tight buttocks, legs together, toes pointed, shoulders shrugged, head between arms, etc. To perform the drill, the athlete uses the abdominal muscles to pull his/her shoulders up off the floor just like he/she did in the crunch drill, but also to pull hi/her legs off the floor at the same time. The movement is a quick snapping motion (See Fig. 28-32). The shoulders and legs come up off the floor at the same time. For a split second, no part of the athlete is touching the floor as the athlete snaps. This is until the lower back and buttocks hit the floor and the athlete rests solely on hi/her lower back and buttocks. The shoulders and legs are only 2-3 inches off the floor, the athlete is looking up at the ceiling, the chin is not tucked to the chest, the legs are tight, toes pointed, and the knees never bend.

Fig 28: Correct start position (tight-arch position)

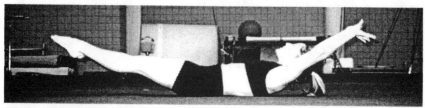

Fig 29: Correct end position (hollow position)

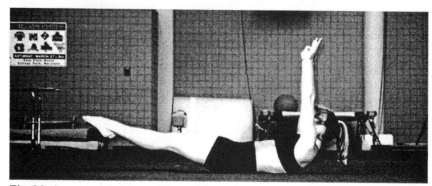

Fig 30: Incorrect finish position; chin and arms are pulled forward

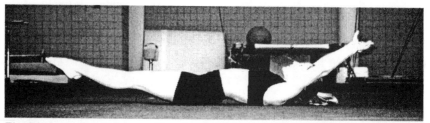

Fig 31: Incorrect finish position; back is arched and shoulders still on ground

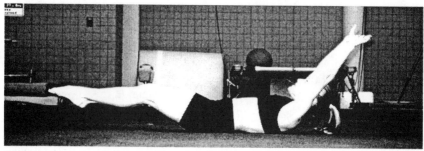

Fig 32: Incorrect finish position; knees bent, shoulder not high enough off floor

The second drill, which is called the <u>shrug drill</u>, is very simple in concept, but is one of the most difficult to do due to the natural tendencies of our bodies and minds. Our bodies try to find ways to cheat to perform movement, in other words to make doing something simple. Unfortunately, it is this natural tendency to cheat which makes learning and doing certain drills and skills more difficult. This is one of those drills. Since this drill is so easy to cheat on, it is very important to ensure the athletes are performing the drill correctly. First, have the athlete face a wall and stand about two feet away from it with his/her arms over the head in a *hollow position* (See Fig. 33). Then the athlete leans towards the wall and places his/her hands on it. The athlete's head is in the *neutral-position* and the body is still in the *hollow position*. Using only the shoulder muscles, the athlete shrugs away from the wall then throws his/her arms back behind the head pulling him/her away from the wall (See Fig. 34-37).

Fig 33:

Fig 34: Correct start position

Fig 35: Position after shrugging off wall

Fig 36: Correct finish position

Fig 37: Incorrect end position; arched back

This is the part where cheating will most likely occur. The body has a natural tendency to use the buttocks to help thrust the body off the wall. This is incorrect and makes the performance of the drill ineffective. Also the athletes have a tendency to want to bend the arms to push away from the wall instead of only using the shoulders (See Fig. 38-40). This is also incorrect.

Fig 38: Incorrect; hips pressed forward

Fig 39: Incorrect; thrusting buttocks back

Fig 40: Incorrect; bending arms to shrug

The next drill, known as the handstand snap-down drill, combines the handstand, the shrug drill, and the snap drill together. To perform this drill, the athletes gets into a handstand, but should be in more of a *tight-arch handstand position* (See Fig. 41). Then the athlete snaps to a *hollow-position* using the abdominal muscles just like in the snap drill, and blocks off the floor just like in the shrug drill. The most common mistake made here is the athlete use the hip-flexors to snap the legs down instead of hi/her stomach muscles to snap the hips down. If an athlete uses hi/her hip-flexors, he/she will be piking down to the floor. This will cause them to land with the chest down and the buttocks sticking up in the air. It's important that the athlete keep his/her buttock's tight and uses the abdominal muscles to snap down with. The athlete wants the feet to land on the floor half of his/her body length away from where the hands were in the handstand (See Fig. 41-46). The athlete's chest, shoulders and arms should be up over his/her legs and feet, facing the wall not the floor and the head should be in the *neutral-position*. Another common mistake that athletes make is, after they block off the floor, they throw their arms down and back so their arms are by their hips. This will bring their chests down instead of up. It is very important that the athlete reaches the arms up and over his/her head after he/she blocks. This will help lift his/her chest up off the floor over the hips.

Fig 41: Correct start position

Fig 42: Position after snapping to hollow

Fig 43: Position after blocking through shoulders

Fig 44 Correct end position

Fig 45: Incorrect end position; arms back, buttocks stuck out and not tight

Fig 46: Incorrect end position; chest and arms down, buttocks stuck out and not tight

The last drill that precedes actually doing the handspring is the dip drill. This is actually the first part of the handspring. The drill is performed by the athlete standing about one foot away from a wall with his/her back towards it. The arms are again over the head and are shrugged, the head is in the *neutral-position*, and the shoulders are directly over the hips. The buttocks is tight and stomach sucked in; they are NOT in a *hollow-position* (See Fig. 47). Leading with his/her buttocks, keeping the shoulders directly over the hips, he/she sits back as if sitting into a chair and falling against the wall. The shoulders and buttocks should hit the wall at the same time (See Fig. 47-50). The two most common mistakes when performing this drill are either leading backwards with the shoulders or leaning forward as he/she sits.

Fig 47: Correct start position

Fig 48: Correct finish position

Fig 49: Incorrect; leaning shoulders back while sitting

Fig 50: Incorrect; sitting w/butt back

Those are the basic drills that should be performed to teach someone how to do a back handspring. These drills need to be done relentlessly until they can be performed consistently with no mistakes, with correct body-position, and with ease. An athlete will tire very quickly with these drills and will easily become bored. This, however, is no excuse for them to not perform these drills repeatedly and correctly. It is one of the necessary evils involved in learning how to tumble. All skills learned after this incorporate these drills and body positions.

Once the athlete has a good solid ability to perform these drills then performing a handspring is a matter of putting several of the above drills together. The first part of the handspring is the dip drill, next the athlete jumps straight up. The most common misconception is he/she needs to jump back. This is not true. The athlete will already be going backwards from the dip. Out of the dip drill, he/she needs to jump so the shoulders go straight up. While doing this, he/she needs to aggressively reach his/her hands backwards behind the head, as he/she did in the shrug drill. It is very important that the athlete keeps the abdominal muscles tight while jumping so the legs and hips come up off the floor over the head. The jump, reach, and tight abs will put the body into a handstand in the *tight-arch position*. This is all dependent upon the athlete keeping his/her entire body tight while being aggressive. Being in a handstand in the *tight-arch position* is the same position needed to perform the handstand snap-down drill, which is exactly what he/she is going to do next. There is one important note while performing the handstand snap-down drill. Instead of thinking about relaxing and then shrugging the shoulders to block up off the floor, the athlete wants to just try and keep the shoulders shrugged as much as possible and push through the shoulders as hard as possible. The block will be almost automatic as long as he/she stays tight and just stays shrugged while pushing through the shoulders. Once he/she snaps down as he/she did in the <u>handstand snap-down drill</u>, he/she will land on the feet in the hollow position, with the chest, shoulders, and arms up over the hips, legs, and feet (See Fig. 51-61).

Fig 51: Correct start position

Fig 52: Correct dip position

Fig 53: Position just after jump

Fig 54: Tight-arch handstand position

Fig 55: Position after snapping hollow

Fig 56: Position after blocking through shoulders

Fig 57: Correct landing position for no rebound

Fig 58: Incorrect landing position; chest down and piked

Fig 59: Incorrect dip position; chest forward and arms down & back

Fig 60: Incorrect handstand; legs apart and bent

Fig 61: Incorrect handstand; arms apart and bent

Fig 62: Correct handstand position

The athlete has just performed a handspring. In performing the handspring, the athlete should travel backwards his/her body length. To determine proper distance for the handspring have the athlete lie on hi/her back and place the arms over the head. Mark where the feet, middle of the stomach and hands are on the floor (See Fig. 63).

Fig 63: Correct distance for hands and feet placement in a back handspring

Have the athlete stand on his/her foot mark. In doing the handspring, the hands should hit where the stomach was, and he/she should land where the hands were while lying on the floor. It is very important that the athlete keeps the arms straight and shoulders shrugged at all times especially in the handstand. They must also keep their buttocks and stomach tight to prevent both arching and piking. *NOTE: It is highly recommended that an athlete first try it with a spot and uses proper mating (SEE SPOTTING for proper spotting technique).*

Throughout the entire learning process several things have been stressed (these points will be used in every drill/skill from this point on):

a) Arms straight
b) Toes pointed
c) Bodies tight
d) Legs together
e) Squeeze both the stomach and the buttocks
f) Head between arms
g) Arms up over the head

The most common areas where an athlete will make mistakes in his/her handspring are:

a) Legs come apart
b) Not keeping the arms straight
c) Arching
d) Landing with the buttocks in the air
e) Throwing the head and shoulders back when jumping
f) Knees bending
g) Reaching the arms down towards the floor as he/she snaps down
h) Not blocking up off the floor with his/her arms and getting the chest, shoulders, and arms up over the lower body
i) Not jumping aggressively

By performing the drills with strict adherence to form, we have made the possibility of doing the handspring without these mistakes a lot more probable. By teaching the body muscle memory with the strict form of the drills, chances are a lot better that when the body puts all the drills together it will remember the strict body form and have less of a tendency to get loose and make those mistakes. It becomes a matter of the body remembering all the drills and putting them together. It will be easier to correct mistakes in the athlete since the body is familiar with the strict form from the drills. Point being, it is easier to refresh body memory than to teach it from scratch and/or overcome bad muscle memory.

BACK TUCKS

Learning a standing back tuck is relatively simple compared to a back handspring. The only prerequisite is that the athlete have a good powerful quick jump. There are really only two main drills to teach a back tuck. This is not to say they are the only drills, but they are the primary ones that teach the basic technique.

The first drill is extremely simple. The straight-jump drill is performed by the athlete standing upright with the buttocks squeezed and stomach tight. The arms are by his/her side. Next the athlete dips down then jumps straight up into the air. (See Fig. 64-66). The athlete should be reaching up over his/her head aggressively which will give him/her extra height and power and will put him/her slightly in a *tight-arch position*. The legs should be straight and not kicked behind them and the head should be between the arms focused slightly up.

Fig 64: Correct start position

Fig 65: Correct dip

Fig 66: Correct jump position

Fig 67: Incorrect; back arched and kicking back

The next drill is called the tuck drill. This drill is performed by having the athlete lie down on his/her back with the arms stretched over the head (same start position as the crunch drill). Next the athlete uses the abdominal muscles to lift the legs, hips, and feet off the floor over his/her head so the toes touch the floor behind the head. This is the finish position. As the legs and feet come up, the arms swing down along the floor to the buttocks then up to grab under the knees and then help pull the legs, hips, and feet over his/her head to the finish position (See Fig. 68-73).

Fig 68: Correct start position

Fig 69: Beginning to tuck

Fig 70: Finishing tuck

Fig 71: Correct end position

Fig 72: Incorrect beginning of the tuck; feet being pulled to buttocks

Fig 73: Incorrect end position; knees tucked to chest

Some mistakes that the athlete will make is:
  a) Pulling the feet to the buttocks before up and over the head
  b) Arching the back
  c) Not using the arms to pull the legs
  d) Pulling the legs to the chest instead of over the head

Performing the back tuck is literally a combination of the two drills. The athlete jumps straight up into the air as in the straight-jump drill. Then at the apex of the jump, he/she does the tuck drill. There are several intermediate drills that can be done to help the athlete put the two drills together. However, most of these require specialized equipment and/or a trained coach. However, there is one intermediate drill that can be done without any specialized equipment.

The jump-tuck drill is very simple and gets the athlete used to combining the two previous drills. First, the athlete jumps into the air just like in the straight-jump drill, when he/she lands on his/her feet, he/she then sits to his/her buttocks, rolls onto the back and tucks just like in the tuck drill. It is important that the athlete keep the arms over the head the entire time, especially while he/she is sitting down onto his/her back. When they land on the back the arms are over the head on the floor. As he/she tucks and pulls the legs up over the head, the arms swing on the floor exactly like the tuck drill. The finish position is also the same (See Fig. 74-83). The most common mistake the athlete makes is bringing the arms forward while sitting down to the floor.

Fig 74: Correct start position

Fig 75: Correct dip position

Fig 76: Correct jump position

Fig 77: Sitting after the jump. Also see Fig 83

Fig 78: Continuing to sit with arms up

Fig 79: Just finished sitting onto floor before the tuck

Fig 80: Starting to tuck

Fig 81: Continuing to tuck

Fig 82: Correct end position

Fig 83: Incorrect sit; chest is forward and arms are down

When the athlete feels comfortable with the drills and is proficient at them, he/she can try to perform the actual standing back tuck itself. To perform the tuck, the athlete simply puts the straight-jump drill and the tuck drill together. As the athlete reaches the apex of the jump, he/she does the tuck drill. He/she stays in the tuck until the feet hit the floor and his/her chest is up facing the wall. Most athletes will have a tendency to come out of the tuck as he/she sees the floor. This is very dangerous. The athlete needs to have enough mental discipline to stay in the tuck and not open up early. By staying in the tuck until he/she sees the wall, he/she will allow the body to rotate enough so he/she will land on the feet and not on the knees or face (See Fig. 84-90). It is recommended that when he/she first attempts this skill, he/she has a spot and uses proper matting (See SPOTTING for proper spotting technique).

Fig 84: Correct start position

Fig 85: Correct dip

Fig 86: Correct jump position

Fig 87: Starting to tuck at apex of jump by pulling knees and feet up

Fig 88: Continuing to pull legs, hips, and feet up and over the body

Fig 89: Continuing to tuck using both arms and abs to pull legs, hips, and feet.

Fig 90: Correct finish position. Chest is up facing the wall and not facing the floor.

The most common mistakeas an athlete will make are:

        a) tucking right off the floor and not finishing the jump

        b) pulling the knees to the chest instead of over the head causing he/she to rotate slowly

        c) opening out of the tuck early and reaching for the floor causing he/she to not fully rotate and land on the knees or face

Another step that can be used in helping an athlete learn the standing back tuck is to get a folded panel-mat. Have the athlete stand on the mat so his/her heels are on the edge. The athlete then does the tuck landing on the floor below the mat. This added height makes the tuck easier. As the athlete gets more proficient at it, gradually unfold the mat so the athlete starts closer to the ground. Eventually he/she will be able to do the tuck on the floor. Again, it is highly recommended the athlete be proficient at the drills and have a qualified spot before attempting this skill.

ROUND-OFFS

A round-off is the basic entry into a backwards tumbling pass. This makes it also the most important skill being performed in the tumbling pass. It can be considered the foundation of any skill performed after the round-off. Just as a bad foundation leads to a bad structure, a bad round-off will lead to a bad tumbling pass.

A round-off can be complicated to learn since there is both a half twist and a flip involved. However, most people find a forward flip easier than a backward one. This is because people have a natural fear of going backwards because one cannot see where he/she is going. Since one can see where one is going in a forward flip, a round-off is mentally easier to learn than a backward skill. There are several ways to learn a round-off. The most common way is a cartwheel.

The first step in a cartwheel is to start in a lunge with the arms raised up over the head. It is important that the athlete's front leg be bent, back leg straight with hips square to the direction he/she is facing. To prevent his/her hips from opening up and not being square, make sure the back foot is facing the direction he/she is and not turned out to the side. (If the athlete has the left leg forward, his/her left shoulder goes forward and the right shoulder goes back as he/she is reaching for the ground. This is called turning to the right. If the right leg is forward then his/her right shoulder goes forward and the left shoulder goes back. This is called turning to the left). It is best that the athlete performs the cartwheel on a straight line. One should start the lunge on the line, place the hands on the line and land with his/her feet on the line. To do a cartwheel, the athlete reaches out in front of him/her towards the ground with the arms. The head should remain between the arms the entire time. One should look at his/her hands but keep the head in-between the arms and the ears by his/her biceps. About half-way to the ground the athlete turns his/her upper body 1/4 of a turn. The hands should remain close together, no more than 6 inches apart. It helps if the athlete makes a picture frame with the thumbs and forefingers and maintains that through out the cartwheel. As he/she is doing the 1/4 turn, the back leg is kicking up and over the head while the front leg pushes off the floor. He/she is now facing 90 degrees from his/her start position in a handstand with the exception of his/her legs not being together. The kicking leg continues towards the floor as the hips rotate another 1/4 turn. As the kicking leg hits the ground the arms push off the floor just like in the back handspring and the shrug drill. As the athlete lands, one is facing the direction he/she came from, and the kicking leg is in front of him/her and is bent, and the leg that pushed off the floor is behind him/her and is straight. One has landed in a lunge, same as the start position but facing the opposite direction (See Fig. 91-97). His/her arms should be over the head. Hand and feet placement, and distance covered is the same as in the back handspring.

Fig 91: Correct start position

Fig 92: Reaching towards floor while kicking

Fig 93: 1/4 turn into handstand (right turn)

Fig 94: Handstand position

Fig 95: 1/4 turn out of handstand

Fig 96: Coming down into lunge with arms and chest up

Fig 97: Correct finish position

Turning a cartwheel into a round-off requires a couple simple changes to the cartwheel. As the athlete lunges and reaches to the floor and kicks, he/she actually kicks into a handstand with the legs together. Just as in the cartwheel, the athlete rotates his/her hips 1/4 turn, but snaps the legs down together as in the handstand snap-down drill. Basically you're using the beginning of the cartwheel to get into a handstand, then the handstand snap-down drill with a 1/4 turn to get out of the handstand (See Fig. 98-104). These are the basics of a round-off. Next the athlete takes a couple steps into the lunge, then finally a run. The keys to the round-off are the same as the other skills discussed previously; mainly tightness, body control, strict adherence to body form, etc. It is best if the athlete performs the round-off on a straight line to ensure he/she placing the hands and feet in the correct place. The distance covered in the round-off is about the same as in the handspring.

Fig 98: Correct start position

Fig 99: 1/4 turn into handstand

Fig 100: Handstand

Fig 101: 1/4 out of handstand and snap down

Fig 102: Hollow body as chest comes up and legs come down

Fig 103: Correct landing position for no rebound

Fig 104: Incorrect landing position; chest down and body piked

NOTE: As stated earlier, the round-off is the most important skill in a tumbling pass. Therefore, the athlete needs to practice and perfect the round-off so it is extremely tight and powerful. The more power an athlete has out of the round-off, the more power he/she will have to use in the skills after the round-off.

ROUND-OFF BACK HANDSPRING

Connecting a round-off and a back handspring together is simpler than it sounds, atleast physically. Mentally it is a very challenging for the athletes. So it is best that the athlete has a strong and powerful round-off and standing back handspring before attempting to connect them.

The first aspect that needs to be understood is what is the difference between a rebound and a jump. A jump involves the athlete bending his/her knees and pushing through the legs and toes to get off the floor. A rebound entails the athletes using physics in its simplest form to get up off the floor, mainly Newton's 3rd law; "For every action there is an equal and opposite re-action." In its simplest form, the reason you do not fall through the floor you're standing on is because the floor is pushing on you with the exact amount of force that you weigh. In other words. If you weigh 100lbs, the floor is pushing back on you with 100lbs of force, so you do not fall through the floor. The trick in a rebound is to make the floor think you weigh 200lbs instead of 100lbs This is accomplished with a little help from gravity and good muscle control.

Let's say you drop a 1 lb rock on the floor, it will bounce a little bit. This is because gravity pulled the rock into the floor with more force than the rock weighs. Basically gravity made the floor think the rock weighed more than it really does. So when the 1 lb rock hits the floor, the floor thinks it weighs 2 lbs. Newton's Law says the floor pushes or hits the rock back with 2 lbs of force. Since the rock only weighs 1 lb and is being pushed on with 2 lbs of force, the rock is pushed up into the air. The rock has rebounded up off the floor.

Lets say you throw the rock into the floor. So now you have gravity and the force you added carrying the rock downward. Now the floor thinks the rock weighs 4lbs and pushes back on it accordingly. The rock will obviously bounce/rebound higher.

Now lets say you do the exact same thing to a lump of soft clay. Wether you drop it or through it at the floor, the clay will barely bounce, if at all. The reason for this is simple. The clay is soft and *loose*, and the rock is hard and *tight*. A loose object will absorb the force given to it by the floor, where as a tight object will be propelled upward by the force. So it is very important that the athlete knows how to stay tight and not bend his/her knees or arms and absorb the force from the floor. By staying tight, an athlete will rebound up off the floor instead of having to jump or push oneself off of it.

The two primary advantages to a rebound compared to a jump is that 1) it is much faster and 2) more powerful. These two advantages are very important in helping athletes perform tumbling passes of any skill level.

In a standing back handspring, the athlete jumps into the skill. In a round-off back handspring, the athlete rebounds into the handspring. The rebound replaces the jump. So when the athlete snaps down in the round-off, it is important that he/she keeps the toes pointed and legs tight. This makes the floor think the athlete weighs more than he/she actually does. This way the floor pushes the athlete up off the floor just like it did with the rock. The harder and faster one snaps and punches the floor with their hands and balls of his/her feet, the harder and faster the floor is going to push one off of it; i.e. the bigger the rebound. If the athlete is loose and bends the knees as he/she punches the floor, the athlete will absorb the force that the floor is applying to him/her. This will prevent the athlete from rebounding just like the lump of soft clay.

So the first step in learning a round-off back handspring is to ensure that the athlete can rebound out of the round-off and standing back handspring. To learn how to rebound, we modify a drill we did earlier, the handstand snap-down drill. We now can call this the rebound drill. Instead of snapping down and landing, the athlete does this drill and tries to rebound. To do this, the athlete snaps the hips and feet under his/her body. Keeping the legs straight and toes pointed, one punches the floor with the balls of the feet. As he/she punches the floor and starts to rebound, the athlete reaches the arms up over his/her head. By staying tight, the floor will punch the athlete up into the air. The athlete has just rebounded straight up. When first trying this drill, it can be very difficult to rebound out of a handstand. So you can have the athlete start the handstand on a slightly raised surface, such as a panel mat. This will make rebounding out of the handstand easier (See Fig. 105-107).

Fig 105: Correct start position

Fig 106: Position just before rebound (feet under hips)

Fig 107: Rebound position (shoulders over, hips over legs)

As one becomes more proficient at the drill, you can gradually lower the panel mat and eventually remove it. To rebound out of the round-off and the back handspring, the athlete simply snaps down and punches the floor the same as he/she did in the rebound drill. Once the athlete has become proficient at snapping down both in the drill, the round-off, and standing handspring, it is time to put everything together. To do this we simply make a minor change to the round-off and add the back handspring. *NOTE: It's very important that the athlete stays tight and does not bend the legs at any time. If one does, the rebound will have very little power and the athlete will most likely have to jump into the next skill to get the power to perform it. Besides this, many bad habits and body positions will develop. Learning a rebound correctly is very important.*

Up to this point, the athlete wants to snap his/her feet and hips directly under the body, not behind or in front of it. This makes the athlete rebound straight up. But, if one snaps his/her hips, legs, and feet a little in front of the body, the rebound will be up and back (See Fig. 108-110). This is the kind of rebound we want out of the round-off for a round-off back handspring. Remember in the standing back handspring, the athlete sat back and jumped up. This caused the athlete to go up and back into the handspring. Since we already established that the rebound replaces the jump, the position that the athlete snaps his/her feet to rebound replaces the dip in the standing back handspring. So by snapping the hips and feet a little bit in front of the body in the round-off, one will rebound up and back into the back handspring.

Fig 108: Snapping the floor, before rebound; feet and hips pressed forward

Fig 109: Position just after rebound; hips and feet forward, arms reaching up

Fig 110: Rebounding up and back; feet and hips in front of shoulders

To snap the hips and feet in front of oneself, the athlete just needs to block of the hands and get his/her chest and shoulders up off the floor faster, snap-down out of their handstand quicker and try to pull the hips and feet in front of him/her more. When he/she is able to do this, he/she will feel his/her rebound go up and back and you will be able to see his/her hips and feet more in front of the bodies as he/she punches the floor.

Once the athlete is able to rebound up and back consistently, to add the handspring the athlete simply reaches back to go into the handstand just like in the standing back handspring (See Fig. 111-113). But he/she is using the rebound to replace their jump and get the legs and feet over his/her body.

Fig 111: Correct snapping position to go into a handspring

Fig 112: Reaching back to the handspring while rebounding up and back

Fig 113: Hitting the handstand for the back handspring

The key to this is that the athlete has a strong and powerful rebound that goes up and back and not just up. As stated earlier, the quicker the athlete blocks the chest and shoulders up off the floor and snaps the hips and feet down into the floor, the quicker and more powerful his/her rebound will be. This is indifferent to what skill they are trying to rebound out off. It is recommended that when an athlete first attempts this skill he/she has a spot and uses proper matting (See SPOTTING for proper spotting technique).

ROUND-OFF/STANDING BACK HANDSPRING BACK TUCKS

NOTE: The first skill a gymnast is taught in a tumbling run is a layout. A layout is the key take-off position for advanced skill performance such as fulls, double fulls, double backs etc. However, this book only covers basic tumbling skills that beginner to intermediate cheerleaders would be using. A layout is considered an advanced skill and not covered in this book.

Assuming the athlete has maintained strict adherence to all the drills and technique up to this point and has good body strength, control, and awareness. Adding a back tuck to the standing handspring or a round-off back handspring is technique wise the same as far as technique goes and should be relatively easy.

Just as in adding a back handspring to the round-off using the rebound to replace the jump, we do the same with adding the tuck to the handspring (whether the handspring is a standing one or out of a round-off). In the standing tuck we wanted the jump to go straight up. Therefore, when the athletes snap down out of his/her handspring, they want to snap the hips and feet directly under the body so the rebound takes them straight up. As in the rebound drill, the athlete needs to get the arms up off the floor over the head and reaching up, not back, aggressively as he/she rebounds, this should put one in the *tight-arch position* just like he/she was when doing the standing tuck. Once in this position, he/she simply does the tuck drill as in the standing tuck (See Fig. 114-119). It is recommended that when an athlete first attempts this skill, he/she has a spot and uses proper matting (See SPOTTING for proper spotting technique).

Fig 114: Tight-arch handstand in back handspring just before snapping to hollow

Fig 115: Snapping to floor out of handspring

Fig 116: Body position on floor just before rebound; feet under hips, rebound will go up

Fig 117: Rebound position reaching up aggressively

Fig 118: Tucking at the apex of the rebound pulling hips and feet up and over shoulders

Fig 119: Correct landing position, chest up feet under body

MULTIPLE BACK HANDSPRINGS

Once the athlete has attained a strong and powerful round-off back handspring, adding another back handspring is extremely simple. Knowing that the snap down in a handspring and the round-off are the same, we can simply modify the snap down in the back handspring just like we did to the round-off. In other words, the athlete simply snaps his/her hips and feet down more in front of him/her in the handspring just like in the round-off. This will rebound him/her up and back just like in the rebound of the round-off. Then the athlete simply goes for the handspring just like he/she did out of the round-off. This technique is used to add any number of handsprings. The most important aspect of a multiple skill tumbling run are solid basics and good technique. The athlete needs to be able to generate power out of the tumbling skills, especially the round-off. So in a multiple handspring tumbling pass, each consecutive handspring should be faster and have more power than the one that preceded it.

GENERAL REMINDERS

As stated at the beginning, this book is written for teams that have access to limited matting, equipment, and professional gymnastics instruction. It in no way represents the only correct way to teach tumbling skills. There are hundreds of different methods and drills that can be used to help and athlete learn how to tumble. The drills contained within this book require the least amount of special equipment and covers the simplest and most basic way to learn tumbling skills. The drills and methods in here will only work effectively if the athletes work on the drills repetitively and often, preferably 3-4 days a week. It also requires that the athlete do the drills with the strictest of form. In may take several months before an athlete has the drills and body control well enough to move onto a handspring or other skills. This does not mean they should not practice the drills associated with that skill. But, it may be a while before they are ready to put all the drills together to perform the skill. Every step in this book requires that the athlete has acquired the previous drill/skill correctly and proficiently. I cannot stress enough that trying to move onto more advanced skills/drills before the previous drills/skills are perfected will impede an athlete's performance, ability to learning it, and could be dangerous to the athlete's physical well-being. Once each drill/skill is perfected, moving onto the next step will be relatively easy.

If an athlete is having problems with a skill/drill, he/she should go back a step or two to the more basic drill/skill and make sure it is perfected and done correctly. Most of the time, a problem in a drill/skill can be corrected by fixing the drill/skill that came before it. An example is that if an athlete has very little power coming out of the handspring and getting to the feet, there are a couple possible reasons for this. Most likely it's in the athlete's jump or snap down, or a combination of the two. Go back and have the athlete redo the drills leading up to the handspring and make sure he/she is doing it correctly. See that he/she is jumping hard and correctly and not throwing the head and/or shoulders back. Also, see that he/she is blocking quickly and powerfully through the shoulders to get the hands and chest up off the floor, and he/she is reaching the arms up and back and not down and back. See that the athlete is doing the *handstand snap-down drill* quickly and powerfully and that he/she is not loose in the stomach and arched. One should be using hi/her abdominal muscles and not the hip-flexors to snap with. Having the athlete re-perform drills will reinforce the correct muscle memory and help the athlete fix the handspring. Keep in mind that putting several drills together to perform a bigger drill/skill will take practice. The more the athletes practice both the individual drills and combination drills, the better the skills performance will be. Basic body control drills and basic skills should be preformed routinely regardless of what level skill the athlete is working on. The better an athletes basics are, the better his/her advanced skills will be.

Make sure your athletes know that learning how to tumble takes a lot of work and dedication and that learning skills will not happen over night. It may take many months to several years to learn some skills. The amount of time an athlete spends working on the drills will determine how long it will take to learn a skill. Some athletes will require different drills not contained within this book and professional gymnastics instruction to attain his/her tumbling goals.

SPOTTING

Spotting an athlete is an extremely important job that should not be taken lightly. The athletes' life is literally in the spotters hands. It is the spotters' job to stop the athlete from getting injured when they make a mistake in performing a skill. The most important area of the body to spot is the head, neck and shoulders. If nothing else, it is extremely important to keep the athletes' head, neck and shoulders from hitting the floor. **Impacts and injuries to these areas of the body are the most serious since paralysis and death can occur from injuries sustained in these areas. If an athlete receives a head or neck injury it is <u>EXTREMELY IMPORTANT that they not be moved or allowed to move and professional medical attention is sought immediately</u>. Premature movement of a person who has sustained a head and/or neck injury can result in further and more severe injuries, including permanent paralysis and death.**

When spotting, it is important that the spotter know what he/she is doing, paying full attention to the athlete performing the skill and be sufficiently strong enough to spot the athlete performing the skill. A spotters primary responsibility is to keep the athlete's head, neck and shoulders from hitting the floor. A spotters secondary responsibilities are to prevent less severe injuries such as broken bones, tendon and ligament tears, sprains, soft tissue injuries such as bruises, black and blue marks etc. It is unacceptable to allow the athlete to be injured in anyway shape or form when spotting them, however, some injuries are more important to prevent than others. In other words, preventing a broken neck is more important than and sprained ankle. If you had a choice between grabbing their legs or head and shoulders when spotting, the head and shoulder would be your primary concern, if the athlete sprains their ankle in doing so, it is less sever than the head and neck injury would be.

<u>NOTE:</u> Proper matting and safety equipment is an integral part of spotting!!!! If you have very little experience spotting, you should practice on an athlete who already has the skill being spotted perfected. This will allow you to get a feel for how to spot without the athlete being in any danger. When first spotting an inexperienced athlete, one should have an experienced spotter spot with you.

BACK HANDSPRINGS

To spot a back handspring, you first need to decide which side of the athlete you feel more comfortable standing on. If you stand on the RIGHT side of the athlete, your going to place your left hand on the small of the athlete's back and your right hand on the back of the right leg just above the knee. If you stand on the athletes' LEFT side, then place your right hand on the small of the back and your left hand on the back of the left leg just above the knee. The fingers of the hand you place on the lower back should be perpendicular to their spine. Never have the fingers or thumb parallel to the spine. The fingers can be broken as the athlete travels backwards. When positioning yourself in relation to the athlete it is important to keep one thing in mind. You are able to support the most weight when the weight is directly in front of you and close to your body. Therefore, when spotting on either side, you should stand about half way between where the athlete is standing and where their hands will land in the handstand. You should not be directly beside them. This is because the athlete will place his/her maximum weight on you right after the jump and just before the hands hit the floor. Since he/she is traveling backwards, you need to be behind him/her so they are right in front of you when he/she places the maximum weight on you. You also want to be as close as possible to the athlete and not arms length away (See Fig. 120-125).

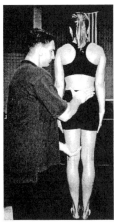

Fig 120: Proper hand placement & distance to the side of the athlete when spotting on the LEFT side.

Fig 121: Correct hand placement. Spotter is lined up behind the athlete to spot.

Fig 122: Incorrect position; lined up directly to the side of the athlete

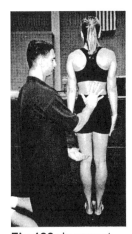

Fig 123: Incorrect hand placement; fingers high up on back.

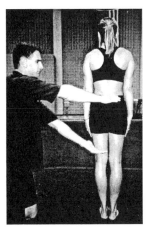

Fig 124: Incorrect position; to far away from the athlete

NOTE: *Due to the height difference between the spotter and the athlete, the spotter in the pictures is on his knees. The height difference between the spotter and the athlete, along with what position the spotter is more comfortable with will determine if they are kneeling or standing while spotting. It is important to note, that standing is a more preferable position while spotting(See Fig. 125). It gives the spotter more mobility and strength while spotting that will help compensate for any unforseen situations that could occur while spotting.*

When spotting the athlete, you use the hand on the lower back to lift them up and the hand on the leg to flip them through the handspring. As the athlete jumps into the handspring, you apply pressure on the back to keep him/her up off the floor. As you do this you take the hand on the leg and lift it up over the waist and finish flipping them over. You want to apply enough pressure on both the back and leg to keep them from hitting their head on the floor and to finish the flip. But, you do not want to lift so hard their hands do not hit the floor or that your throwing the athlete through the skill. You want to only apply sufficient power so the athlete does not become injured, but does much of the skill themselves. You are primarily there just incase he/she makes a mistake, not to do it for them.

Fig 125: Proper position to the side of the athlete while standing to spot

BACK TUCKS

Spotting a back tuck is almost exactly the same as spotting the back handspring with a few minor differences. The first one, which is actually very serious, is that the athlete is not in contact with the floor while performing the skill. So unlike the handspring the athlete has no way to lesson the impact of the hitting the floor if they bail out of the skill. It is extremely important that the spotter be strong enough to support the athletes entire body weight. This will allow the spotter to stop the athlete from hitting the floor if they bail on the skill. As in the back handspring, the spotter uses one hand to support the athletes body and the other to flip the athlete. Another difference in spotting is that the athletes' jump should be straight up and down and not travel back. So you want to stand more on the side of them but still a little behind them (See Fig. 126).

A technique that will allow you more control of the athlete while spotting them is to take your hand on their lower back, twist their shirt so its tight around their body and hold onto the shirt while the do the skill (See Fig. 127).

ROUND-OFF BACK HANDSPRING

The spotting of this skill requires good timing and hand-eye coordination. It requires you to step in just as the athlete snaps down in the round-off. The spotting of the handspring itself is the same as in the standing back handspring. However, you need to be able to get your hands on the athlete just as their feet hit the floor before they rebound. This is the difficult part of the spot. Stand approximately where their feet will land in the round-off. As they snap their feet down in the round-off, place your hands in the correct places on his/her body and spot them. You need to be comfortable enough with getting close to the athlete as he/she is flipping and getting your hands in on the athlete at the right time to spot. Standing far away from him/her and spotting will not work and is very dangerous to the athlete. As with spotting standing skills. You need to be close to them to be effective.

Fig 126: Correct position in relation to the athlete

BACK HANDSPRING BACK TUCK

Whether the handspring is a standing one or out of the round-off, spotting the tuck is exactly the same. The technique for spotting the tuck is the same as in the standing back tuck. Just like in the round-off back handspring, you need to get your hands onto the athlete just as the feet hit the floor but before the rebound. Stand approximately where the feet will hit the ground out of the handspring. As they are snapping down out of the handspring, you need to step close into the athlete and place your hands in the correct positions on the body to spot. As stated before you need to be comfortable stepping in and getting close to the athletes as they are flipping. Standing far away from them and trying to spot is very dangerous and ineffective.

Fig 127: Grabbing the shirt technique

NOTE: It cannot be stressed enough how very important it is that the person spotting an athlete has the proper training and experience in spotting. It is strongly discouraged that a person with very little spotting experience be allowed to spot an athlete who does not have a skill by themselves. It is also recommended that when first spotting a new athlete, there is a second experienced spot just in case. Only after a lot of practice and experience should one attempt top spot someone on their own.

NOTES

NOTES

NOTES

NOTES

NOTES

NOTES

NOTES

NOTES